POWER PRESSURE COOKER XL COOKBOOK

Over 40 detailed recipes that help you prepare delicious & healthy meals

Contents

INTRODUCTION

The Power Pressure Cooker XL are the next trendy kitchen additions. People are happy about these products' efficiency and convenience. A typical pressure cooker that uses electric power contains an inner pot. This pot has different sizes, which determine how big or small the outer casing would be. Usually, their holding capacities range from three to six liters. This does not mean that you cannot find larger inner pots.

These are available, but at a higher price. To ensure durability, manufacturers make some inner pots with stainless steel and clad their bottoms with copper. This ensures consistent heating when using the electric cooker. In addition, a person who would rather pay less money can get a model with an aluminum inner vessel. The only problem it would give him or her is cleaning, because aluminum is usually not dishwasher safe.

You can easily remove the pan and return it without any hassles. Another feature that your electric pressure cooker would have is a lid with a tight sealing gasket. When fastened, the lid and the inner pot create a very airtight compartment. When you connect the pressure cooker to the power supply, the inner-pot would warm up. This heat then increases the pressure inside it. If the lid were not tight enough, the pressure being generated in the compartment would force it up.

This is why some manufacturers prefer a special lock mechanism involving a float valve with a pin. As the swelling pressure pushes up the lid, the pin exerts more tightness. It works in a similar manner as the latch lock. As you explore the pressure cooker market, you will notice some differences in the construction of the lid lock. Safety is a major consideration when one is cooking with any electric or gas appliance.

Most pressure appliances have high-tech safety valves and pushdown pressure release systems. You can find very innovative safety mechanisms on many modern instant pots. All the items that utilize a float valve with pin are secure, but not necessarily in the long run. At some point, large amounts of heat and pressure generation could destroy the pin. Once the pin functionality fails, then it means that the lid would not sustain itself in a locked position, if pressure mounts excessively in the inside vessel.

Additionally, you can find some cookers that use a pressure release-regulating valve. This would only let go of excess pressure when the pot is in use and sealed. Another major feature that this equipment has is a heating element situated on the outer casing. It also consists of a control box with a role of regulating heat and pressure of the inside vessel. It controls both temperature and pressure sensors because it has a microprocessor. Moreover it has a timer to help you prepare food properly.

It would warn you if something goes wrong by producing some sound. Most electric pressure cookers models operate at a pressure range of about seventy-to eighty-kilopascal. This is equivalent to a heat range of about 239 to 244 degrees F. That is why it is q uick and it is able to save your time. With this cooking appliance, you can prepare broccoli, dry beans, corns, and other related foods. It would only take two minutes of your time to prepare vegetables. The dry legumes might take extra time.

BLACK BEAN STEW

Servings 4

Ingredients
2.5 cup Black beans, dry

5 cup cups water (for quick soak or overnight soak)

1.5 cup onion, chopped

5.5 cup green bell pepper, chopped

3 clove garlic, chopped fine

1 tablespoon salt

0.25 teaspoon black pepper

2 tablespoon olive oil for sautÃ©ing

1 teaspoon oregano

0.5 teaspoon cumin, ground

1 bay leaf

1 ounce vinegar

2.5 cup water (for cooking)

2 ounce dry white wine

2 teaspoon sugar

2 tablespoon olive oil (to drizzle over beans in final step)

Directions
1. Cover dry beans with water and let stand covered overnight. Drain and discard water.

2. Quick soak method: cook dry beans in the pressure cooker with 5 cups of water for 10 minutes, drain water. Follow recipe below.

3. Place the inner pot into the Pressure Cooker.

4. Place the soaked black beans in to the inner pot. Add water and 1 tbsp. olive oil â˘' this will prevent the beans from foaming.

5. Place the lid on the Power Pressure Cooker XL, lock the lid and switch the pressure release valve to closed.

6. Set the time to 5 minutes. Press the BEANS/LENTILS button.

7. Once the timer reaches 0, the cooker will automatically switch to KEEP WARM. Press the CANCEL button. Switch the pressure release valve to open. When the steam is completely released, remove the lid.

8. Remove the beans from the inner pot. Or sautÃ© next steps in a pan. Do not drain the water from the cooked beans.

9. SautÃ© the onions, garlic and green pepper in olive oil until the onions are translucent.

10. Add the oregano, cumin, and bay leaf. This makes your Sofrito.

11. Add this Sofrito to the beans, add the sugar, vinegar, wine, salt and pepper.

12. Place the lid on the Pressure Cooker, lock the lid and switch the pressure release valve to closed.

13. Press the BEANS/LENTILS button then TIME ADJUSTMENT button. Set the time to 10 min.

14. Once the timer reaches 0, the cooker will automatically switch to KEEP WARM. Press the CANCEL button. Switch the pressure release valve to open. When the steam is completely released, remove the lid.

15. Press the SLOW/COOK button. Default is 2 hours, but let simmer for at least 30 minutes with lid off. (this step is optional, but it combines the flavors)16. Serve the prepared black beans over white rice.

CLASSIC CUBAN BEEF STEW

Servings 4

Ingredients

4   medium potatoes â€" peeled, diced large

1 pound beef cut into large cubes (top round)

0.5   white onion large diced

0.25   green pepper medium diced

3 clove garlic minced

0.5 teaspoon cumin

1 tablespoon oregano

8 ounce tomato sauce

8 ounce diced tomato

4 ounce water

6 ounce dry white wine

1   bay leaf

2 ounce vegetable oil

0   Salt and pepper to taste

Directions

1. Place the inner pot into the Pressure Cooker. Place the oil in the inner pot. Press the MEAT/CHICKEN button.

2. Saute the beef in the oil in small batches until browned on all sides. Remove and reserve beef.

3. Saute the onion, pepper and garlic. Cook until translucent. Add white wine reduce by half. Add remaining ingredients cumin, oregano, tomato sauce, diced tomato, bay leaf, water, potatoes, and beef. Mix ingredients.

4. Place the lid on the Pressure Cooker, lock the lid and switch the pressure release valve to closed. Press the MEAT/CHICKEN button. Press the TIME ADJUSTMENT button until you reach 20 minutes.

5. Once the timer reaches 0, the cooker will automatically switch to KEEP WARM. Press the CANCEL button. Switch the pressure release valve to open. When the steam is completely released, remove the lid.6. Serve with white rice.

WHITE RICE

Servings 4

Ingredients

2 cup long grain white rice

16 ounce water

1 teaspoon oil

0 PINCH OF SALT (OPTIONAL)

Directions

1. Place the inner pot into the Pressure Cooker.

2. Add the rice, water, oil and salt.

3. Press the RICE/RISOTTO button once to select White (6 minutes).

4. Place the lid on the Pressure Cooker, lock the lid and switch the pressure release valve to closed.

5. Once the timer reaches 0, the cooker will automatically switch to KEEP WARM. Press the CANCEL button. Let the steam naturally release. When the steam is completely released, remove the lid.6. Fluff rice with a fork and serve.

BROWN RICE

Servings 4

Ingredients

2 cup brown rice

18 ounce water

1 teaspoon oil

0   Pinch of salt (optional)

Directions

1. Place the inner pot into the Pressure Cooker.

2. Add the rice, water, oil and salt.

3. Press the RICE/Risotto button. To select Brown. Press the TIME ADJUSTMENT button until you reach 18 minutes.

4. Place the lid on the Pressure Cooker, lock the lid and switch the pressure release valve to closed.

5. Once the timer reaches 0, the cooker will automatically switch to KEEP WARM.

6. Press the CANCEL button. Let the steam naturally release. When the steam is completely released, remove the lid.

7. Fluff rice with a fork and serve.

CHICKEN SOUP

Servings 4

Ingredients

5   chicken thighs, skin removed

1   medium potatoes, peeled and cut into large pieces

2   carrots cut in large half inch half moons

1   ear of corn, cut in 1 inch wheels

2   tomatoes, diced

1   onion, diced

2 clove garlic, minced

2   stalks of celery, diced

1   bay leaf

9   chicken stock

1 tablespoon Sea Salt

1 teaspoon pepper

0.5 cup chopped parsley

Directions
1. Place the inner pot into the Pressure Cooker.

2. Add all the ingredients into the inner pot.

3. Press the SOUP/STEW button, then the time select button set to 30 minutes

4. Once the timer reaches 0, the cooker will automatically switch to KEEP WARM. Press the CANCEL button. Let the steam naturally release. When the steam is completely released, remove the lid.

5. Add the parsley and serve.*With this amount of ingredients in the pressure cooker it may take up to 20 minutes to pressurize. Then let the steam naturally release, so liquid is not released from the pressure valve.

CARROT GINGER SOUP

Servings 4

Ingredients

2.5 pound carrots large diced

2 tablespoon ginger fresh, peeled, chopped,

3 tablespoon olive oil

1 cup chopped onion

2 clove garlic minced

4 cup chicken or vegetable broth

1 cup dry white wine

0.25 teaspoon freshly ground black pepper Sea Salt

3 tablespoon unsalted butter

4 ounce milk

Directions
Place the inner pot into the Pressure Cooker.

Add all the ingredients from group one into the inner pot.

Press the SOUP/STEW button, then the time select button set to 30 minutes

Once the timer reaches 0, the cooker will automatically switch to KEEP WARM. Press the CANCEL button. Let the steam naturally release. When the steam is completely released, remove the lid.

Carefully puree the ingredients. Add in the ingredients from group two

Then serve.

ROASTED RED PEPPER SOUP

Servings 4

Ingredients

6   red bell peppers â€"cut thick julienned

2   red onions â€"cut thick julienned

4   plum tomatoes â€"cut thick julienned

2 clove garlic minced

1   potato peeled, diced

6 cup chicken stock

1 cup white wine (Chardonnay)

2 tablespoon olive oil

1 tablespoon Sea Salt

1 teaspoon White Pepper

Directions

Place the inner pot into the Pressure Cooker.

Place the oil in the inner pot. Press the Soup/Stew button. Set time to 15 min

Add the red peppers, garlic and onion. Cook until they get soft 3-4 minutes then add tomatoes, and white wine cook additional 2-3 minutes

Add the chicken stock and potato

Place the lid on the Pressure Cooker, lock the lid and switch the pressure release valve to closed.

Once the timer reaches 0, the cooker will automatically switch to KEEP WARM. Press the CANCEL Button. Switch the pressure release valve to open. When the steam is completely released, remove the lid.

APPLE CIDER PORK LOIN

Servings 4

Ingredients

2 pound Center-cut Pork Loin

2 tablespoon olive oil

2 cup Cider

1   Medium onion, sliced

2   Apples, cored and sliced

1 tablespoon Sea Salt

1 tablespoon Freshly ground black pepper

1 tablespoon Minced dry onion

Directions
Season the pork loin with salt, pepper and minced dry onions.

Place the inner pot in the cooker. Place the olive oil in the inner pot.

Press CHICKEN/MEAT button sear the pork loin on all sides.

Remove and set aside. Saute the onions.

Add the remaining ingredients and the pork loin.

Place the lid on the Power Pressure Cooker XL, lock the lid and switch the pressure release valve to closed.

Press the CANCEL button.

Press the CHICKEN/MEAT button and then TIME ADJUSTMENT to 20 minutes.

Once the timer reaches 0, the cooker will automatically switch to KEEP WARM. Press the CANCEL Button. Switch the pressure release valve to open. When the steam is completely released, remove the lid.

Serve.

MASHED SWEET POTATOES

Servings 4

Ingredients

4   sweet potatoes, peeled and sliced

1.5 cup water

0.25 cup maple syrup

2 tablespoon butter

0.5 tablespoon Sea Salt

0.25 tablespoon Freshly ground black pepper

Directions

Place the inner pot inside the cooker.

Add the water and the sweet potatoes.

Place the lid on the Power Pressure Cooker XL, lock the lid and switch the pressure release valve to closed.

Press the SOUP/STEW button. Set to 10 minutes.

Once the timer reaches 0, the cooker will automatically switch to KEEP WARM. Press the CANCEL Button. Switch the pressure release valve to open. When the steam is completely released, remove the lid.

Remove the cooked sweet potatoes from the water. Place them in a bowl add the remaining ingredients and mash together until desired consistency.

Serve.

LEG OF LAMB WITH HERBS

Servings 4

Ingredients

1   boneless leg of lamb

3   sprigs rosemary leaves, removed and chopped

1 tablespoon black pepper, ground

3 tablespoon olive oil

1 pound brussel sprouts, cleaned and trimmed

1 pound baby red and yellow potatoes

2   carrots, peeled and cut into 6

2 cup beef stock

2 tablespoon flour

2 tablespoon butter

Directions

Combine the herbs and garlic. Place the lamb fat side down on the cutting board. Rub the inside of the lamb with half of the herb mixture. Season with salt and pepper.

Roll the lamb and tie it with butcherâ€™s twine to hold into a roll. Place the rest of the herb mixture on top of the roast and season with salt and pepper.

Place the inner pot into the Power Pressure Cooker XL. Place the olive oil in the inner pot. Press the CHICKEN/MEAT button. Brown the roast on all sides.

Press the CANCEL button. Place the lid on the Power Pressure Cooker XL, lock the lid and switch the pressure release valve to closed.

Press the CHICKEN/MEAT button. Set time to 10 minutes.

Once the timer reaches 0, the cooker will automatically switch to KEEP WARM. Press the CANCEL Button. Switch the pressure release valve to open. When the steam is completely released, remove the lid.

Add the potatoes and vegetables.

Place the lid on the Power Pressure Cooker XL, lock the lid and switch the pressure release valve to closed.

Press the CHICKEN/MEAT button. Set time to 10 minutes.

Once the timer reaches 0, the cooker will automatically switch to KEEP WARM. Press the CANCEL Button. Switch the pressure release valve to open. When the steam is completely released, remove the lid.

Remove and reserve the lamb and vegetables.

Make a paste with the flour and butter. Then press the CHICKEN/MEAT button.

Add the stock to the inner pot and bring to a boil. Stir in the flour butter paste. Cook for about 10 minutes.

Slice the meat. Heat up the vegetables and potatoes in the sauce.

the pork loin with salt, pepper and minced dry onions.

Place the inner pot in the cooker. Place the olive oil in the inner pot. Press CHICKEN/MEAT button sear the pork loin on all sides. Remove and set aside. Sautà© the onions.

Add the remaining ingredients and the pork loin.

Place the lid on the Power Pressure Cooker XL, lock the lid and switch the pressure release valve to closed.

Press the CANCEL button.

Press the CHICKEN/MEAT button and the n TIME ADJUSTMENT to 20 minutes.

Once the timer reaches 0, the cooker will automatically switch to KEEP WARM. Press the CANCEL Button. Switch the pressure release valve to open. When the steam is completely released, remove the lid.

Serve.

CHOCOLATE STEAM PUDDING

Servings 4

Ingredients
1 cup All purpose flour

1 tablespoon Baking Powder

4 teaspoon Cocoa Powder

0.5 cup Butter, room temp.

0.75 cup Brown Sugar

2 Eggs

0.5 cup Heavy Cream

1 tablespoon Vanilla Extract

6 ounce Melted dark chocolate

0.5 cup Heavy Cream

1 cup Chocolate chips, semi-sweet

Directions

In a medium size bowl, mix the butter and sugar together. Mix in one egg at a time, then flour until incorporated. Mix in the chocolate and the rest of the ingredients.

Spray the pudding pan with non-stick spray.

Spoon the pudding into steam pudding pan and place the lid on the pan.

Place the inner pot in the cooker. Set the wire rack in the inner pot. Pour 2 cups of warm water into the pot of the cooker Place the steam pudding pan into the inner pot.

Place the lid on the Power Pressure Cooker XL, lock the lid and switch the pressure release valve to closed.

Press the SOUP/STEW button. Set time to 10 minutes.

Once the timer reaches 0, the cooker will automatically switch to KEEP WARM. Press the CANCEL Button. Switch the pressure release valve to open. When the steam is completely released, remove the lid.

Carefully remove the pudding pan from the cooker and cool for 2 hours.

Remove the lid, place a plate on the top and turn over. Remove the pan from the plate.

Empty and clean the inner pot. Place back in the cooker.

Press the CHICKEN/MEAT button. Add the cream, bring to a boil. Press the CANCEL button, and stir in the chips until smooth to make the glaze.

Pour the glaze over the chocolate steamed pudding.

Slice and serve.

CRANBERRY ORANGE BREAD PUDDING

Servings 4

Ingredients

4   Egg yolks

3 cup Brioche, cubed

2 cup Half & half

1   Orange, zested and juiced

0.5 tablespoon Vanilla

0.75 cup sugar

2 tablespoon Butter, Soft

0.75 cup Cranberries

Directions

In a medium size bowl, mix the eggs, cranberries, zest, orange juice, sugar, half & half, and vanilla extract.

Soak the cubed brioche in the egg mixture for 10 minutes.

Pour mixture into a 6-inch baking dish and cover with foil or 3 smaller ramekins.

Place the inner pot into the Power Pressure Cooker XL. Set the wire rack in the inner pot. Pour 2 cups of warm water into the inner pot of the cooker. Place the baking dish on the rack in the cooker.

Place the lid on the Power Pressure Cooker XL, lock the lid and switch the pressure release valve to closed.

Press the CHICKEN/MEAT button. Set time to 15 minutes.

Once the timer reaches 0, the cooker will automatically switch to KEEP WARM. Press the CANCEL Button. Switch the pressure release valve to open. When the steam is completely released, remove the lid.

Carefully remove the Bread Pudding from the cooker and remove the foil.

Cool before serving.

PUMPKIN CHEESECAKE

Servings 4

Ingredients

0.5 cup cooked pumpkin

2 cup cream cheese

0.75 cup sugar

1 tablespoon cinnamon

2 Eggs

0.5 tablespoon Vanilla Extract

1 cup graham cracker crust

0.25 cup sugar

2 tablespoon melted butter

Directions

In a bowl combine the sugar, graham cracker crumbs and the butter. Place the crust in a 6-inch cheesecake pan and press the crumbs to form a crust on the bottom of the pan.

Place the cream cheese and the sugar in a bowl. Mix with an electric mixer. Mix in one egg at a time. Mix in the rest of the ingredients.

Pour mixture into the cheesecake pan.

Completely wrap the pan foil.*

Place the inner pot into the cooker. Pour 1 cup of warm water into the inner pot. Place the steaming rack inside the inner pot.

Place the cheesecake pan into the cooker.

Place the lid on the Power Pressure Cooker XL, lock the lid and switch the pressure release valve to closed.

Press the CHICKEN/MEAT button. Press TIME ADJUSTMENT until you reach 20 minutes.

Once the timer reaches 0, the cooker will automatically switch to KEEP WARM. Press the CANCEL Button. Switch the pressure release valve to open. When the steam is completely released, remove the lid. Carefully remove the cheesecake from the cooker.

Remove the foil. Chill in the refrigerator for 2 hours.

Once the cheesecake has set remove from the pan and serve.

PUMPKIN SOUP WITH PUMPKIN SEEDS

Servings 4

Ingredients

2 cup cooked pumpkin

1 cup Cider

5 cup chicken stock

1 cup Heavy Cream

1   Cinnamon stick

3   Apples cored, q uartered

1 tablespoon Nutmeg

1 tablespoon Sea Salt

2 tablespoon butter

1   Onion, peeled and diced

1   Carrot, peeled and diced

1 cup Pumpkin seeds, toasted

Directions

Place the inner pot into the Power Pressure Cooker XL. Place the butter in the inner pot. Press the CHICKEN/MEAT button.

Add the carrots and onions. Cook 10 minutes.

Add the rest of the ingredients except for the cream and pumpkin seeds, stir well. Press the CANCEL button.

Place the lid on the Power Pressure Cooker XL, lock the lid and switch the pressure release valve to closed.

Press the SOUP/STEW button. Set time to 10 minutes.

Once the timer reaches 0, the cooker will automatically switch to KEEP WARM. Press the CANCEL Button. Switch the pressure release valve to open. When the steam is completely released, remove the lid.

Stir in the cream.

Serve and garnish with toasted pumpkin seeds.

SHRIMP BISQUE

Servings 4

Ingredients

2 pound Shrimp, peeled cut into small pieces (save the shells)

2 tablespoon Tomato paste

3 tablespoon Flour, all purpose

0.5 cup Heavy Cream

0.5 Stalk celery, minced

1 Onion, peeled and minced

1 Shallot, peeled and minced

3 Sprigs tarragon

2 Sprigs thyme

3 tablespoon Sherry

4 cup water

0 Sea salt and pepper to taste

Directions

Place the inner pot into the Power Pressure Cooker XL. Place the butter in the inner pot. Press the CHICKEN/MEAT button.

Add the shrimp shells, onions, celery, carrots and shallots and stir occasionally for about 4 minutes. Add the flour and tomato paste and cook for 2 minutes.

Add the rest of the ingredients except cream, shrimp and sherry. Bring to simmer until thickened 3-4 minutes.

Place the lid on the Power Pressure Cooker XL, lock the lid and switch the pressure release valve to closed.

Press the SOUP/STEW button. Set time to 10 minutes.

Once the timer reaches 0, the cooker will automatically switch to KEEP WARM. Press the CANCEL Button. Switch the pressure release valve to open. When the steam is completely released, remove the lid.

Strain out the shells and vegetable. Reserve the liquid and return to the inner pot.

Add the dice shrimp, cream and sherry to the soup.

Press the CHICKEN/MEAT button. Stir. Simmer for 2 minutes to cook shrimp and marry the flavors.

Season with sea salt and freshly ground black pepper.

SPAGHETTI SAUCE

Servings 4

Ingredients

2 can crushed tomatoes

0.5 cup water

3   cloves garlic, minced

1 tablespoon oregano, fresh chopped

1 tablespoon Sea Salt

2 tablespoon olive oil

Directions

Place the Inner pot in the Power Cooker. Press the BEEF/CHICKEN button and sautÃ© the onions and garlic in the olive oil. Add tomatoes and the rest of the ingredients and let cook for 5 min.

Carefully ladle the sauce into the jars 1" from the top.

Using a flexible nonporous spatula gently press between the sauce and the jar to release any trapped air bubbles.

Clean the rims with white vinegar and seal.

Place the jars into the clean inner pot and add water until the jars are covered 1/4 of the way.

Secure the lid, close the steam release valve and press the CANNING/PRESERVING button and then press the COOK TIME SELECTOR button until it reaches 45 min.

When the time runs out and the steam has been released, remove the lid and carefully remove the jars using the canning tongs.

HARD BOILED EGGS

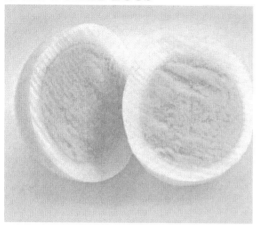

Servings 4

Ingredients

12   Eggs

1.5 cup water

0   Wire rack

   0 Large bowl filled half way with ice and water (ice bath)

Directions

Place the inner pot into the Pressure Cooker.

Push the Rice/Risotto button. 6 min.

Put the wire rack. Add the water.

Place the Lid on the cooker, lock Lid and switch the Pressure Valve to Closed.

Once the timer reaches 0, the cooker will Automatically switch to KEEP WARM. Switch the Pressure Valve to Rapid Release. When the steam is completely released, remove the Lid.

Care remove eggs and place it the ice bath, let the eggs cool for a few minutes and peel.

Serve

APPLE SAUCE

Servings 4

Ingredients

8   Apples, cored and halved

0.5 cup sugar

0.5   Cinnamon stick

0.5 cup water

Directions

Place all the ingredients into the inner pot.

Press the FISH/VEGETABLE button for 4 minutes.

When the steam has released remove the lid and mash the applesauce.

Carefully ladle the applesauce into the jars 1" from the top.

Using a flexible nonporous spatula gently press between the applesauce and the jar to release any trapped air bubbles.

Clean the rims with white vinegar and seal.

Place the jars into the clean inner pot and add water until the jars are covered 1/4 of the way.

Press the CANNING/PRESERVING button and then press the TIME ADJUSTMENT button two times until you reach 20 minutes.

When the time runs out and the steam has been released, remove the lid and carefully remove the jars using the canning tongs.

CHILI STARTER

Servings 4

Ingredients

4 cup crushed tomatoes

0.5 cup beef stock

1 Large onion, peeled and diced

0.333333 cup Dried red beans

0.333333 cup Black beans

0.25 cup Chili powder

1 tablespoon cumin

1 tablespoon Ground coriander

1 tablespoon Crushed red pepper flakes

1 tablespoon sugar

2 tablespoon Grape seed oil

Directions

Place the inner pot into the Power Cooker. Place the oil in the inner pot. Press the CHICKEN/MEAT button. Sauté the onions for 5 minutes. Add the spices and cook for an additional minute.

Add the remaining ingredients. Place the lid on the pressure cooker, lock lid and switch the pressure release valve to closed.

Press CANCEL and then press the SOUP/STEW button.

Once the timer reaches 0, the cooker will automatically switch to KEEP WARM. Switch the pressure release valve to open. When the steam is completely released, remove the lid.

Carefully pour into the jars 1â€ from the top.

Using a flexible nonporous spatula gently press between the chili and the jar to release any trapped air bubbles.

Clean the rims of the jars with white vinegar.

Place the lids on the jars.

Place the jars into the clean inner pot and add water until the jars are covered 1/4 of the way.

Secure the lid, close the steam release valve and press the CANNING/PRESERVING button and then press the COOK TIME SELECTOR button until you reach 45 min.

When the time runs out press the CANCEL button and then the CANNING/PRESERVING button and the time will be 30 min.

When the time runs out and the steam has been released, remove the lid and carefully remove the jars using the canning tongs.

To finish the chili brown 2 lbs of ground meat and follow the instructions in the pressure cooker recipe book for beef chili

EASTER HAM

Servings 4

Ingredients

10 pound Ham

0.5 cup Brown Sugar

30 Whole cloves

1 cup Pineapple juice

1 cup Brown mustard

Directions

Place the inner pot into the Power Pressure Cooker XL.

In a bowl mix all the ingredients together except the ham and whole cloves.

With a paring knife carve thin lines down the ham to place the whole cloves Â½ inch apart.

Pour half the mixture into the inner pot and place the ham side down.

Place the lid on the Power Pressure Cooker XL, lock the lid and switch the pressure release valve to closed.

Press the CHICKEN/MEAT button and then the COOK TIME SELECTOR twice until the time says 1 hour.

Once the timer reaches 0, the cooker will automatically switch to KEEP WARM. Press the CANCEL Button. Switch the pressure release valve to open. When the steam is completely released, remove the lid.

Remove the ham from the inner pot. Reserve the glaze for later use.

Slice ham and serve. Pour glaze over sliced ham.

KING CRAB

Servings 4

Ingredients

4 pound King Crab Legs

1 cup water

0.25 cup melted butter

3 Lemon wedges

Directions

Break the crab legs in half at the joints to fit into the Power Cooker.

Place the inner pot into the Power Cooker.

Add the water and crab legs.

Place the lid on the Power Cooker, lock the lid and switch the pressure release valve to closed.

Press the FISH/VEGETABLE button and then press the TIME ADJUSTMENT button until you reach 3 Min.

Once the timer reaches 0, the cooker will automatically switch to KEEP WARM. Switch the pressure release valve to open. When the steam is completely released, remove the lid.

Serve with melted butter and lemon wedges.

COQ AU VIN

Servings 4

Ingredients
4   Chicken thighs and legs

0.25 cup Potato starch

1 cup Red wine, preferably pinot noir (marinate chicken)

0   Sea salt and freshly ground black pepper

6 ounce Slab bacon, cubed

1   medium onion, q uartered

2 cup red wine, preferably pinot noir

8 ounce Button mushrooms, quartered

2   stalks, celery, large dice

2   medium carrots, large half moon cut

24   Pearl onions

6   Petite yellow potatoes

2 tablespoon Tomato paste

3 clove garlic, crushed

3   Sprigs fresh thyme

1   bay leaf

1 tablespoon Sea Salt

Directions
You can use frozen pearl onions and defrost in the refrigerator over night. Since they will be braised the flavor will hold.

Marinate the chicken in the red wine at least one hour - best over night.

Remove chicken from the Red wine pat dry, Season chicken with salt and pepper, roll it in Potato starch

Place the inner pot into the Pressure Cooker. Press the Soup/Stew button. Press the Time adjust button to Set time to 20 min.

Heat oil and cook bacon slowly until crispy. Remove and reserve bacon. Cook chicken in the same oil until golden brown on each side. Remove a reserve.

Add more oil if needed: add the quartered onions, and garlic cook 2-3 minutes. Add the red wine into the inner pot, and reduce 3-4 minutes. Add, Chicken stock everything from group 4 stir, then everything from group 3 and return bacon and chicken.

Place the lid on the Pressure Cooker, lock the lid and switch the pressure release valve to closed.

Once the timer reaches 0, the cooker will automatically switch to KEEP WARM. Press the CANCEL Button. Switch the pressure release valve to open. When the steam is completely released, remove the lid.

Serve a chicken thigh or leg and portion of each of the vegetables with some of the sauce.

Serve

PENNE IN MEAT SAUCE

Servings 4

Ingredients

1 pound ground beef

2 pound Dry penne

3 cup water

3 cup Marinara sauce

1 cup Ricotta

10 ounce Shredded mozzarella cheese

1 tablespoon salt

0.5 Onion diced

3 clove garlic minced

1 tablespoon black pepper

2 ounce olive oil

Directions

Place the inner pot into the Pressure Cooker. Press the Rice/Risotto button. Set time to 8 min.

Heat the oil and cook the beef til browned, add the onion and garlic, drain away excess fat.

Place the sauce and the water in the inner pot.

Add the Penne, salt and pepper mix well with a large spatula.

Place the lid on the Pressure Cooker, lock the lid and switch the pressure release valve to closed.

Once the timer reaches 0, the cooker will automatically switch to KEEP WARM. Press the Cancel button. When the steam is completely released, remove the lid.

Add ricotta, and mozzarella. Mix gently with large spatula and Serve.

CANNED PEACHES

Servings 4

Ingredients

10   Peaches

2 cup water

0.75 cup sugar

Directions

To peel peaches: Bring a pot of water to a boil. Make an X with a knife to score the peach on the bottom. Place the peaches into the boiling water. After 2 minutes place the hot peaches into an ice bath. The skin should remove easily. Cut the peaches in half and place them in the jars.

To make the syrup: Place the sugar and water into the inner pot and press the CHICKEN/MEAT Button. Bring to a boil for a couple of minutes.

Pour the syrup into the jars of peaches 1" from the top.

Using a flexible nonporous spatula gently press between the peaches and the jar to release any trapped air bubbles.

Clean the rims with white vinegar and seal.

Place the jars into the clean inner pot with water 1/4 of the way up the jars.

Secure the lid and close the steam release valve.

Press the CANNING/PRESERVING button and the TIME ADJUSTMENT until you reach 20 minutes.

When the time runs out and the steam has been released, remove the lid and carefully remove the jars using the canning tongs.

CANNED PEARS

Servings 4

Ingredients

6   Pears peeled,cored

0.75 cup sugar

2 cup water

Directions

To make the syrup: Place the sugar and water into the inner pot and press the CHICKEN/MEAT Button. Bring to a boil for a couple of minutes.

Cut the pears into quarters and place into the jars. Carefully pour the syrup into the jars 1â€ from the top.

Using a flexible nonporous spatula gently press between the pears and the jar to release any trapped air bubbles.

Clean the rims with white vinegar and seal.

Place the jars into the clean inner pot and add water until the jars are covered 1/4 of the way.

Press the CANNING/PRESERVING button and then press the TIME ADJUSTMENT button two times until you reach 20 minutes.

When the time runs out and the steam has been released, remove the lid and carefully remove the jars using the canning tongs.

DILL PICKLES

Servings 4

Ingredients

10   Pickling cucumbers

6 clove Garlic, smashed

2 cup water

2 cup White vinegar

0.25 cup Sea Salt

1 bunch Fresh dill

1 tablespoon Pickling spice

4 us liquid pint Jars

Directions

Pour the water, vinegar, half the salt, pickling spice and dill into the inner pot and press the CHICKEN/MEAT button. Bring to a boil.

Cut the pickles into spears. Place them into the jars.

Strain the spices out of the brine. Carefully pour the brine into the jars 1" from the top and seal.

Using a flexible nonporous spatula gently press between the pickles and the jar to release any trapped air bubbles.

Clean the rims with white vinegar and seal.

Place the jars into the clean inner pot and add water until the jars are covered 1/4 of the way.

Press the CANNING/PRESERVING button.

When the time runs out and the steam has been released, remove the lid and carefully remove the jars using the canning tongs.

ROASTED RED PEPPER SOUP

Servings 4

Ingredients

6   Red bell peppers-cut thick julienned

2   Red onions- cut thick julienned

4   Plum tomatoes- cut thick julienned

2 clove Of garlic minced

1   potato peeled, diced

6 cup chicken stock

1 cup Of white wine (Chardonnay)

2 tablespoon olive oil

1 tablespoon Sea Salt

1 tablespoon White Pepper

Directions

Place the inner pot into the Pressure Cooker. Place the oil in the inner pot. Press the Soup/Stew button. Set time to 15 min.

Add the red peppers, garlic and onion. Cook until they get soft 3-4 minutes then add tomatoes, and white wine cook additional 2-3 minutes.

Add the chicken stock and potato.

Place the lid on the Pressure Cooker, lock the lid and switch the pressure release valve to closed.

Once the timer reaches 0, the cooker will automatically switch to KEEP WARM. Press the CANCEL Button. Switch the pressure release valve to open. When the steam is completely released, remove the lid.

Carefully remove soup from the inner pot and transfer to blender to puree until smooth. Or use a stick blender.

Serve.

SMOTHERED PORK CHOPS

Servings 4

Ingredients

4   Pork chops, bone in1

1   Garlic clove, minced

3 tablespoon parsley, chopped

2 tablespoon Lime juice

1 pound onions, julienned

0.5 cup milk

1 tablespoon salt

0.5 tablespoon pepper

2 tablespoon olive oil

2 tablespoon butter

1 tablespoon flour

2 tablespoon Cornstarch plus 3 tbsp. of water to make a slurry

0.5 cup White wine

Directions

Place the inner pot into the Pressure Cooker.

Place the oil in the inner pot. Press the CHICKEN/MEAT button. 15 minutes.

Season the pork chops with salt and pepper, Sauté each pork chop until golden brown on each side, Remove pork chops and reserve.

Sauté the onions and garlic until translucent. Add the white wine, and lime juice, Stir the slurry to the onions. Add the milk. Mix gently until thickened. Put the pork chops in the onions.

Place the lid on the Pressure Cooker, lock the lid and switch the pressure release valve to closed.

Once the timer reaches 0, the cooker will automatically switch to KEEP WARM. Press the CANCEL button. Switch the pressure release valve to open. When the steam is completely released, remove the lid.

Remove pork chops and reserve.

Serve pork chops, and then top each one with a portion of onion sauce.

Serve.

CHICKEN TIKKA MASALA

Servings 4

Ingredients

1.5   Pounds boneless, skinless chicken thighs

0.25 cup Plain whole-milk Greek-style yogurt

2 teaspoon Lemon juice

1   Large clove garlic, minced

1 tablespoon Ground coriander

0.5 teaspoon Ground cumin

0.5 teaspoon Ground cardamom

0.5 teaspoon Ground nutmeg

1.5 clove Paprika

0.5 teaspoon Cayenne

1 tablespoon Grated peeled fresh ginger (From 1-inch piece)

4 tablespoon Half stick of unsalted butter

1 Large white onion, finely chopped

20 ounce Tomato purée (canned)

1.25 teaspoon Kosher Salt

0.5 teaspoon Freshly ground black pepper

0.5 cup Chopped fresh cilantro plus additional sprigs for garnish

Directions

Marinate the Chicken in the yogurt and garlic. Marinate for 1-2 hour overnight is better.

In a small bowl, whisk together the coriander, cumin, cardamom, nutmeg, paprika, cayenne, and ginger.

Place the inner pot into the Pressure Cooker. Press the Soup/Stew button. Set time to 15 min.

Melt the butter. Add the onion, and sauté, stirring occasionally, until light brown and caramelized, about 5 minutes. stir in the spice and ginger mixture. Add the tomato purée, and salt, and bring the sauce to a boil.

Gently simmer the sauce, uncovered, until thickened slightly, about 5 minutes.

Add in the yogurt-marinated chicken.

Place the lid on the Pressure Cooker, lock the lid and switch the pressure release valve to closed.

Once the timer reaches 0, the cooker will automatically switch to KEEP WARM. Press the CANCEL Button. Switch the pressure release valve to open. When the steam is completely released, remove the lid.

Serve.

MOO SHU PORK

Servings 4

Ingredients

2 tablespoon Sesame oil

3 tablespoon Rice wine

1 pound Pork chops boneless, loin cut into strips

1   Large onion; thinly sliced

1 ounce Bag coleslaw mix; shredded

4 ounce Fresh shiitake mushroom stems removed and sliced

1 tablespoon Garlic; minced

0.5 teaspoon White Pepper

0.25 cup beef stock

3 tablespoon Soy sauce

3 ounce Hoisin sauce

4   Scallions; thinly sliced

2 tablespoon Cornstarch; mixed into 2 tablespoons water

0 Moo Shu pancake (substitute flour tortillas)

Directions

Place the inner pot into the Pressure Cooker. Press the Bean/lentil button. Set time to 5 min.

Wait for oil to get very hot. Place the pork and onion in the cooker and cook until pork is lightly browned, about 5 minutes.

Add the coleslaw mix, garlic, beef broth, and soy sauce.

Place the lid on the Pressure Cooker, lock the lid and switch the pressure release valve to closed.

Once the timer reaches 0, the cooker will automatically switch to KEEP WARM. Press the CANCEL Button. Switch the pressure release valve to open. When the steam is completely released, remove the lid.

Stir in hoisin sauce, scallions, and cornstarch mixture. Let simmer 2 minutes.

Serve wrapped in tortillas, spread with additional hoisin sauce if desired.

VEGETABLE PULAO

Servings 4

Ingredients

2 cup Basmati rice (rinsed 3 times)

1 cup Mixed vegetable frozen (carrots peas corn green beans)

2 cup water

0.5 teaspoon Green chill fresh-minced

0.5 teaspoon Ginger fresh minced

3 clove garlic minced

2 tablespoon butter

1   Cinnamon stick

1 tablespoon Cumin seeds

2   Bay leaves

3   Whole cloves

2   Whole cardamoms

5   Whole black peppercorns

1 tablespoon Sea Salt

1 tablespoon sugar

Directions

Place the inner pot into the Pressure Cooker.

Heat the oil and group #1 sautÃ© until fragrant, about 1 min then add in group #2.

Add the rice, water, and mixed vegetables.

Press the RICE/RISOTTO button once to select White (6 minutes).

Place the lid on the Pressure Cooker, lock the lid and switch the pressure release valve to closed.

Once the timer reaches 0, the cooker will automatically switch to KEEP WARM. Press the CANCEL button. Let the steam naturally release. When the steam is completely released, remove the lid.

Fluff rice with a fork.

Serve.

BRUSSELS SPROUTS

Servings 4

Ingredients

1.5 pound Cleaned Brussels sprouts cut in half long ways

6 ounce Sweet soy

2 ounce Rice wine

2 clove Garlic sliced thin

2 tablespoon Canola Oil

1 tablespoon White Pepper

Directions

Place the Inner Pot in the Pressure Cooker. Place the Oil in the Inner Pot. Press BEANS/LENTIL button. Add the grape seed oil and garlic. Cook for 1 minute.

Add remaining ingredients.

Place the Lid on the cooker, lock Lid and switch the Pressure Valve to Closed.

Press CANCEL then press the FISH/VEGETABLE/STEAM button increase the cook time to 5 minutes.

Once the timer reaches 0, the cooker will automatically switch to KEEP WARM. Open the Pressure valve. When the steam is completely released, remove the Lid and press CANCEL.

Serve.

MOROCCAN CHICKEN

Servings 4

Ingredients

4   Chicken quarters (thigh)

3   Onion sliced

24 ounce Dice tomato (Canned)

1 tablespoon Caraway seeds

0.5 cup chicken stock

0   Potato Starch for coating chicken

1 tablespoon Cardamom powder

1 tablespoon Cumin powder

1 tablespoon Coriander powder

1 tablespoon Sea Salt

1 tablespoon black pepper

0 Canola Oil

Directions

Place the inner pot into the Pressure Cooker. Press the Chicken/Meat button. Set time to 15 min.

Heat oil and sear each leg one or two at a time until golden brown. Remove chicken and reserve.

Add the onions and cook until they start to turn color, then add the caraway seeds, dice tomato, chicken stock the remaining spices.

Then bury the chicken under the onions and tomatoes.

Place the lid on the Pressure Cooker, lock the lid and switch the pressure release valve to closed.

Once the timer reaches 0, the cooker will automatically switch to KEEP WARM. Press the CANCEL Button. Switch the pressure release valve to open. When the steam is completely released, remove the lid.

Serve a portion of chicken with tomato and onion mixture.

Serve.

GUMBO

Servings 4

Ingredients
8 ounce Andouille sausage, cut into 1/4-inch thick slices

1.5 pound Skinned boneless chicken thighs

1 pound Medium shrimp

2 cup chicken stock

0 vegetable oil

6 ounce All purpose flour

1 Medium onion, chopped

0.5 Green bell pepper,chopped

2 Celery ribs, diced

3 clove garlic, minced

2 tablespoon FilÃ© powder

2 Bay leaves

1 tablespoon Worcestershire sauce

2 teaspoon Old bay seasoning

0.5 teaspoon Teaspoon dried thyme

0.5 To 1 teaspoon hot sauce

4 Green onions, sliced reserve half for garnish

Directions

Place the inner pot into the Pressure Cooker. Press the Soup/Stew button. Set time to 15 min.

Add oil cook sausage and chicken until browned. Set aside.

Add enough oil to drippings in to measure 1/2 cup. Add flour, and cook, stirring constantly, 2-3 minutes.

Stir in onion, bell pepper, and celery; cook, stirring often, 2-3 min Add Chicken stock chicken, sausage and remaining ingredients.

Place the lid on the Pressure Cooker, lock the lid and switch the pressure release valve to closed.

Once the timer reaches 0, the cooker will automatically switch to KEEP WARM. Press the CANCEL Button. Switch the pressure release valve to open. When the steam is completely released, remove the lid.

Serve.

SOUTH WEST BEEF AND RICE

Servings 4

Ingredients

1 pound ground beef

1   Red onion diced

0.5   Green pepper diced

2 ounce olive oil

10 ounce Dice tomatoes

6 ounce Corn Kernel

8 ounce Cooked black beans (drained)

3   Diced jalapeño

3   cup White Rice

3   cup chicken stock

3   tablespoon Chili powder

1   tablespoon Sea Salt

1   tablespoon pepper

2   ounce Chopped Cilantro

Directions

Place the inner pot into the Pressure Cooker. Press the RICE/Risotto button. 6minutes.

Heat oil and sear beef, drain away excess fat. Season with chili powder, salt and pepper.

Add the onions, garlic, green peppers, and jalapeno, and cook for 2 min.

Add in the Rice and Chicken stock.

Place the lid on the Pressure Cooker, lock the lid and switch the pressure release valve to closed.

Once the timer reaches 0, the cooker will automatically switch to KEEP WARM. Press the CANCEL button. Let the steam naturally release. When the steam is completely released, remove the lid.

Fluff rice with a fork.

Serve.

MUSHROOM RISOTTO

Servings 4

Ingredients
 2 cup Arborio Rice (Risotto)

4 cup Stock

2 clove garlic minced

1   Onion diced

2 ounce olive oil

4 ounce Heavy Cream

2 tablespoon Grated parmesan cheese

1 ounce Basil â€"fresh, chiffonade

8 ounce Crimini Mushrooms

4 ounce Sherry

Directions

1. Place the inner pot into the Pressure Cooker. 2. Push the Rice/Risotto button. Adjust time to 8 min.3. Heat the olive oil, sweat the onions and garlic 2min add mushrooms cook 3 min.4. Add the Rice, Sherry and stock mix to evenly distribute mushrooms.5. Place the Lid on the cooker, lock Lid and switch the Pressure Valve to Closed.6. Once the timer reaches 0, the cooker will Automatically switch to KEEP WARM. Switch the Pressure Valve to Rapid Release. When the steam is completely released, remove the Lid.7. Pour the heavy cream into the rice mixture and fold in parmesan cheese and basil.8. Serve.

PICKLED BEETS

Servings 4

Ingredients

6   Small beets, cooked, peeled & sliced

0.5   Onion, sliced

0.25 cup Cup sugar

1 tablespoon Pickling spice

2   tablespoon Sea Salt

Directions

Place the inner pot into the pressure cooker. Press the CHICKEN/MEAT button and add all the ingredients except the beets.

Bring to a boil.

Pack the sliced beets into the jars.

Carefully pour the liquid and onions into the jars 1â€ from the top.

Using a flexible nonporous spatula gently press between the beets and the jar to release any trapped air bubbles.

Clean the rims with white vinegar and seal.

Place the jars into the clean inner pot and add water until the jars are covered 1/4 of the way.

Secure the lid close the pressure release valve.

Press the CANNING/PRESERVE button.

When the time runs out and the steam has been released, remove the lid and carefully remove the jars using the canning tongs.

TURKEY WITH APRICOT GLAZE

Servings 4

Ingredients

11 pound Turkey

1.5 cup chicken stock

0.5 teaspoon Freshly ground black pepper

1   Large onion, peeled and diced

1   large carrot, diced

6 ounce apricots marmalade

0.5 teaspoon cumin

0.5 teaspoon coriander

0.5 teaspoon tumeric

1 teaspoon salt

1 teaspoon pepper

Directions

Mix ingredients for glaze together to make a paste.

Rinse turkey and pat dry with paper towels.

Rub glaze over Turkey.

Place the Inner Pot into the Pressure Cooker.

Add stock and vegetables to the Inner Pot. Place the turkey breast on top.

Secure the Lid on the Pressure Cooker. Lock the Lid and switch the Pressure Release Valve to Closed.

Press the CHICKEN/MEAT button, and then the COOK TIME SELECTOR button. The time will be set for 40 minutes.

Once the timer reaches 0, the Pressure Cooker will automatically switch to KEEP WARM. Press CANCEL. Switch the Pressure Release Valve to Open. When the steam is completely released, remove the Lid.

Carefully remove the turkey breast from the Inner Pot.

Optional: Place turkey on the lower rack in the oven. Broil until golden brown.

GRANDMA'S MEATBALLS

Servings 4

Ingredients

1 can crushed tomatoes

0.5 cup Cup water

0.5 Onion diced

3 clove garlic, minced

1 tablespoon Basil chopped

1 tablespoon Sea Salt

0.5 tablespoon Fresh ground pepper

1 tablespoon sugar

2 tablespoon olive oil

4 pound ground beef

4 Large eggs

0.5 cup cup milk

0.5 cup Parmigiano cheese

1 cup bread crumbs

3 clove garlic minced

1 Onion minced

1 teaspoon Sea Salt

1 teaspoon Freshly ground black pepper

Directions

To make meatballs, add all meatball ingredients to a bowl and mix. Roll meat balls to desired size and place on a baking sheet. Place in the oven to sear at 450Â° for 10 Min .

Place the inner pot in the Power Cooker. Press the CHICKEN/MEAT button. SautÃ© the onions and garlic in the olive oil. Add tomatoes and the rest of the ingredients and let cook for 5 Min .

Add the seared meatballs.

Place the lid on the Power Cooker, lock the lid and switch the pressure release valve to closed.

Press the WARM/CANCEL button.

Press the SOUP/STEW button and then press the TIME ADJUSTMENT button until you reach 20 Min .

Once the timer reaches 0, the cooker will automatically switch to KEEP WARM. Switch the pressure release valve to open. When the steam is complctely released, remove the lid.

Serve.

SHORT RIBS

Servings 4

Ingredients

8   Short ribs, trimmed

2   Cups, beef stock

1   Medium onion, peeled and diced

2   Stalks celery diced

3   Cloves garlic, peeled and minced

2 tablespoon Tomato paste

8   Red potatoes, small

2 tablespoon olive oil

1 tablespoon Sea Salt

1 tablespoon Freshly ground black pepper

1 Sprig thyme

1 Sprig rosemary

1 bay leaf

Directions

Season the short Ribs with salt and pepper. Pour the olive oil into the inner pot and press the CHICKEN/ MEAT button. Place the ribs into the inner pot and brown on all sides.

Remove the ribs and keep aside. Add the vegetables and garlic and sautÃ© for 4 minutes add the paste.

Place the ribs back in the pot with the rest of the ingredients.

Place the lid on the Power Cooker, lock the lid and switch the pressure release valve to closed.

Press the WARM/CANCEL button.

Press the SOUP/STEW button and then press the TIME ADJUSTMENT button until you reach 40 Min .

Once the timer reaches 0, the cooker will automatically switch to KEEP WARM. Switch the pressure release valve to open. When the steam is completely released, remove the lid.

Serve.

MINI RIGATONI BOLOGNESE

Servings 4

Ingredients

2 tablespoon olive oil

1 pound ground beef

1   Medium onion, peeled, finely chopped

2 clove Garlic, peeled and minced

1   Medium carrot, peeled and finely chopped

0.75 cup Beef broth

0   Pinch cayenne pepper

6 tablespoon Finely grated Parmigiano-Reggiano

1 pound Mini rigatoni pasta

0   Sea salt & freshly ground black pepper to taste

16 ounce tomato puree

Directions

Place the inner pot in the Power Cooker. Place the oil in the inner pot. Press the RICE/RISOTTO button. Place the beef in the pot. Stirring occasionally while cooking.

After 5 minutes add the onion, garlic, carrots and cook until the time is up.

Add the remaining ingredients except the Parmigiano.

Place the lid on the Power Cooker, lock the lid and switch the pressure release valve to closed.

Press the WARM/CANCEL button.

Press the BEANS/LENTILS button.

Once the timer reaches 0, the cooker will automatically switch to KEEP WARM. Switch the pressure release valve to open. When the steam is completely released, remove the lid.

Serve with Parmigiano-Reggiano.

TURKEY SOUP

Servings 4

Ingredients

2 cup turkey meat, diced

6 cup turkey stock

1 cup pastina

1 Large onion, peeled and diced

2 carrots, diced

2 celery stalks, diced

3 Garlic Cloves

2   sprigs, thyme

2 teaspoon salt

0.75 teaspoon Black Ground Pepper

1 pinch poultry seasoning to taste

Directions

Place the Inner Pot into the Pressure Cooker.

Press the SOUP/STEW button. Set time to 10 minutes.

Combine all ingredients in Inner Pot.

Secure the Lid on the Pressure Cooker. Lock the Lid and switch the Pressure Release Valve to Closed.

Once the timer reaches 0, the Pressure Cooker will automatically switch to KEEP WARM. Press CANCEL. Switch the Pressure Release Valve to Open. When the steam is completely released, remove the Lid.

Serve.

THANKSGIVING STUFFING

Servings 4

Ingredients

2   baguette, cut into cubes

8 ounce ground sausage

3   stalks celery, diced

0.5   medium onion, diced

8 ounce mushroom, q uartered

1   large carrot, diced

0.5 cup chicken stock

4 ounce butter

1.5 teaspoon poultry seasoning

1 teaspoon thyme, chopped

1 tablespoon parsley, chopped

0.5 teaspoon salt

0.5 teaspoon Freshly ground black pepper

Directions

Place the Inner Pot into the Pressure Cooker.

Press the SOUP/STEW button to set for 10 minutes.

Melt butter. Add ground sausage. SautÃ© until brown.

Add vegetables. SautÃ© for 4 minutes. Add seasonings.

Add stock and Fold in cubed baguette.

Secure the Lid on the Cooker. Lock the Lid and switch the Pressure Release Valve to Closed.

Once the timer reaches 0, the Cooker will automatically switch to KEEP WARM. Press the CANCEL button. Switch the Pressure Release Valve to Open. Do not remove Lid until steam is released completely.

Serve or

Optional: Transfer to an oven safe dish and bake in oven for 20 minutes at 400 degrees for added crispness.

SWEET POTATOES CASSEROLE

Servings 4

Ingredients

3 pound sweet potatoes, peeled and cut into quarters

1.5 cup water

0.5 teaspoon salt

0.25 teaspoon Freshly ground black pepper

Directions

Place the Inner Pot into the Pressure Cooker. Add water, sweet potatoes salt and pepper.

Secure the Lid on the Pressure Cooker. Lock the Lid and switch the Pressure Release Valve to Closed.

Press the SOUP/STEW button to set for 10 minutes.

Once the timer reaches 0, the Pressure Cooker will automatically switch to KEEP WARM. Press CANCEL. Switch the Pressure Release Valve to Open. When the steam is completely released, remove the Lid.

Mash sweet potatoes adjust seasoning with salt and pepper if needed.

For marshmallow-pecan topping:1 Â½ oz. all-purpose flour (about 1/3 cup)2/3 cup packed brown sugar2 Tbsp. butter, meltedÂ½ cup pecans, chopped2 cups mini marshmallows

After mashing sweet potatoes, transfer into an oven-safe casserole dish.

In a small bowl, add melted butter, brown sugar, and flour. Mix. Fold in pecans.

Spread mixture over sweet potatoes. Top with marshmallows.

Bake at 400Â°F in the oven for 10 minutes or until marshmallows are caramelized.

TURKEY POT PIE

Servings 4

Ingredients

2 cup cooked turkey meat

2 cup chicken or turkey broth

2   potatoes, diced large

2   carrots, peeled and diced

0.5 cup peas

1   Onion, peeled and diced

3 tablespoon butter

3 tablespoon flour

1   bay leaf

1   Sprig thyme

1   stalk celery, diced

1   sheet puff pastry (from freezer section of the grocery store)

1   egg yolk

2 tablespoon milk

Directions

Place the Inner Pot into the Pressure Cooker and press the MEAT/CHICKEN button to set for 10 minutes.

SautÃ© onions and celery in butter.

Stir in flour and let cook for 1 minute. Stir in stock until mixture thickens. Add remaining ingredients except puff pastry, egg yolk, and milk.

Secure the Lid on the Pressure Cooker. Lock the Lid and switch the Pressure Release Valve to Closed.

Once the timer reaches 0, the Pressure Cooker will automatically switch to KEEP WARM. Press CANCEL. Switch the Pressure Release Valve to Open. When the steam is completely released, remove the Lid.

Pour the pot pie mixture into a casserole dish. Place the puff pastry over the mixture. Remove any excess dough. Make three slits in the center of the puff pastry.

Mix egg yolk and milk together. Brush the egg mixture onto the dough.

Place the pot pie into a 350-degree oven for about 10-15 minutes until golden brown.

TURKEY STOCK

Servings 4

Ingredients

1   Turkey carcass with wings or legs

2   carrots, cut in quarters

1   onion, cut in quarters

2   celery stalks, cut in q uarters

1   sprig thyme, whole

2   Bay leaves

1 tablespoon whole peppercorns

6 cup water

0   turkey drippings

Directions

Place the Inner Pot into the Pressure Cooker.

Place turkey carcass into the Pressure Cooker with the rest of the ingredients. Add enough liq uid to cover turkey but do not exceed the max fill line.

Secure the Lid on the Pressure Cooker. Lock the Lid and switch the Pressure Release Valve to Closed.

Press the SOUP/STEW button and then the COOK TIME SELECTOR to set for 30 minutes.

Once the timer reaches 0, the Pressure Cooker will automatically switch to KEEP WARM. Press CANCEL. Switch the Pressure Release Valve to Open. When the steam is completely released, remove the Lid.

Strain stock, discarding bones and vegetables.

APPLE CAKE

Servings 4

Ingredients
2   Granny Smith Apples, cored and diced

1   stick butter, softened

0.666667 cup sugar

1 cup yogurt

2   Eggs

0.5 cup chopped walnuts

1 teaspoon baking soda

1 teaspoon Baking Powder

2 cup all-purpose flour

0.25 cup Brown Sugar

1 teaspoon Vanilla Extract

2 cup warm water

Directions
In a mixing bowl, combine butter and white sugar until smooth.

Add eggs and yogurt. Mix.

Add diced apples and remaining dry ingredients except brown sugar. Mix until creamy.

Butter a ceramic dish that will fit into the Cooker.

Arrange apple on the bottom of the ceramic dish. Sprinkle chopped walnuts and brown sugar over the apples.

Carefully pour batter over the apples.

Cover the dish with foil.

Place the Inner Pot into the Pressure Cooker.

Place the Wire Rack into the Inner Pot. Add 2 cups of water. Place the ceramic dish on the Rack.

Secure the Lid on the Cooker. Lock the Lid and switch the Pressure Release Valve to Closed.

Press the CHICKEN/MEAT button and then the COOK TIME SELECTOR button until the time reads 20 minutes.

Once the timer reaches 0, the Pressure Cooker will automatically switch to KEEP WARM. Press CANCEL. Let the pressure release naturally. Switch the Pressure Release Valve to Open. When the steam is completely released, remove the Lid.

Let cool 15 minutes before serving.

CHOCOLATE PEPPERMINT STEAM PUDDING

Servings 4

Ingredients

1 cup all-purpose flour

1 teaspoon Baking Powder

0.25 teaspoon salt

4 tablespoon Cocoa Powder

0.5 cup butter, room temperature

0.75 cup Brown Sugar

2 Eggs

0.5 cup Heavy Cream

1 teaspoon Vanilla Extract

6 ounce melted chocolate, dark

1 teaspoon candy cane, finely ground

Directions

Glaze:Â½ cup heavy cream1 cup chocolate chips, semi-sweet
Topping:Â½ cup candy cane, finely ground

In a medium bowl, mix butter and sugar together. Add one egg at a time along with flour until incorporated. Mix in chocolate and remaining ingredients.

Spray the steam pudding pan with non-stick spray.

Spoon the pudding into the pan and cover with a lid.

Place the Inner Pot into the Pressure Cooker. Set the Wire Rack in the Inner Pot. Pour 2 cups of warm water into the Inner Pot of the Pressure Cooker. Place the pan on the Rack in the Pressure Cooker.

Secure the Lid on the Pressure Cooker. Lock the Lid and switch the Pressure Release Valve to Closed. Press the SOUP/STEW button to set for 10 minutes.

Once the timer reaches 0, the Pressure Cooker will automatically switch to KEEP WARM. Press CANCEL. Switch the Pressure Release Valve to Open. When the steam is completely released, remove the Lid.

Empty and clean the Inner Pot. Replace inside the Cooker.

To make the glaze:

Press the MEAT/CHICKEN button. Add cream and bring to a boil. Turn the machine off and stir in chocolate chips.

Carefully remove the pudding from the Cooker and let cool for 2-3 hours. Remove the Lid. Hold a plate on top of the pan and turn over. Remove the pan from the plate and sprinkle a generous amount of candy cane powder over the cake. Drizzle glaze over cake.

GLAZED CARROTS

Servings 4

Ingredients

2 tablespoon butter, unsalted

16 ounce baby carrots

4 ounce molasses

2 ounce water

1 teaspoon salt

0.5 teaspoon pepper

2 tablespoon dill, chopped

2 ounce butter

Directions

Place the Inner Pot into the Pressure Cooker.

In the Inner Pot, combine carrots, molasses, salt, pepper, and water.

Secure the Lid on the Pressure Cooker. Lock the Lid and switch the Pressure Release Valve to Closed.

Press the FISH/VEGETABLE button to set for 2 minutes.

Once the timer reaches 0, the Pressure Cooker will automatically switch to KEEP WARM. Press CANCEL. Switch the Pressure Release Valve to Open. When the steam is completely released, remove the Lid.

Strain carrots. Add butter to Inner Pot to melt (it will still be warm). Add carrots and dill. Toss delicately.

Serve with freshly cracked pepper.

Made in United States
Troutdale, OR
07/16/2023

11303436R00066